Which Native Fern?

A Simple Guide to
the Identification of
New Zealand Native Ferns

Andrew Crowe

VIKING

Acknowledgements

Many people went out of their way to help with aspects of this book. In particular I would like to thank Alan Esler (retired DSIR botanist), Dr John Braggins (Senior Lecturer in Botany, University of Auckland), John Smith-Dodsworth (botanical author), Sandra Vandermast (specialist fern propagator) and James Beever (author of *A Dictionary of Maori Plant Names*).

Two of my friends, Gudrun Lellek and Claire Paterson, offered their useful services as 'guinea pigs'; I'd like to thank them for helping to identify 'bugs' in the keys and other pitfalls.

I would also like to thank my editors, Christine Moffat and Bernice Beachman, for their support and helpful criticism, Richard King for his design and copy-editing, Sandra Parkkali for her detailed art, and the army of people who did their best to rescue me from all the system errors, crashed disks, etc., on my Apple Mac.

As a reliable and much-used source of information, I owe a great debt to the excellent, up-to-date and complete reference on the subject, *New Zealand Ferns and Allied Plants*, by Patrick Brownsey and John Smith-Dodsworth.

Andrew Crowe

Using This Book

Before using the frond keys

Although there are many useful specialist terms for describing ferns and parts of ferns, this book keeps to words that are part of everyday language.

Frond = the leaf of a fern (including its stalk)
Leaflet = the smallest division of a frond
Spore = the dust-like 'seed' of a fern

It is useful, too, to understand a few basic concepts before using the keys.

First, the general way in which a fern grows. Whether it is a

tufted fern   **creeping fern**   **climbing fern**   **perching fern**   or a **tree fern**

Second, the basic frond shape or pattern. Whether it is

simple   **once-divided**   or **more than once-divided**

or

Third, the type of edge the leaflet has. Whether it is

untoothed   **toothed**   or **lobed**

Using the frond keys

1. Find a typical frond of a common adult fern. Don't pull it off, because you'll later need to look at how it grows on the fern. Now turn to page 5. (Remember to start at the bottom of the chart.) Then turn to the page indicated.
2. Starting from the arrow at the bottom of this new page, follow the appropriate branches until you arrive at an illustration of your frond. Now turn to the page indicated for a photograph of the fern and a frond silhouette.
3. Just to be sure, run down the checklist next to the photograph and check the sketch of the way in which it grows and how big it gets.

Using the fern pages

Ferns that look similar appear on facing pages. Use the identification checklists on these pages to distinguish between them. These graphics are used.

A guide to the latitudinal limits within which the wild fern is usually found.

A guide to the altitudes where the fern naturally grows (in metres).

The common shape, habit and height of the mature fern, with either an adult person or a copy of this book next to it to give scale.

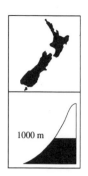

1000 m

Beneath the colour photo is a life-sized silhouette of part of the frond and, in some cases, a life-sized circular photo of a section of the underneath of a frond to show how the spore cases are arranged on that particular fern.*

Common names

It is often said that Māori only named useful plants or that many plant names were made up to please curious Pākehā. This theory was very effectively put to the test by Baron Huegal. In 1834, he made a collection of 300 plants and asked one Māori man to name them. Although many of the plants were small and insignificant, he named all of them. The following evening, another man was invited to do the same. He, too, named all 300. All but one plant received the same name as had been given the night before.

Names (whether Māori or not) do, however, vary from region to region. For simplicity, only the commonest are used here.**

The correct pronunciation of Māori vowels is as follows: a as in far, e as in bet, i as in me, o as in awe, u as in moon. To help with pronunciation, macrons have been included; these indicate a lengthened vowel, e.g., ā = aa.

---

*   Indeed, the arrangement of these is so central to fern identification that it will later become necessary to appreciate that these 'spore cases' or 'spore patches' are, in fact, sori. A sorus consists of many tiny brown capsules, called sporangia. It is in these sporangia that the microscopic spores (usually 64 spores per sporangia) are actually contained. A protective flap, called an indusium, often covers and protects the sorus.

** With the exception of waterfall fern (*Blechnum colensoi*) and sweet brake (*Pteris macilenta*), all the common Māori and European names used in this book have at least one published precedent. Māori names (where a choice exists) are those favoured by James Beever. Those not listed by Beever are from Dobbie (3rd edition) or Potts (see Selected References).

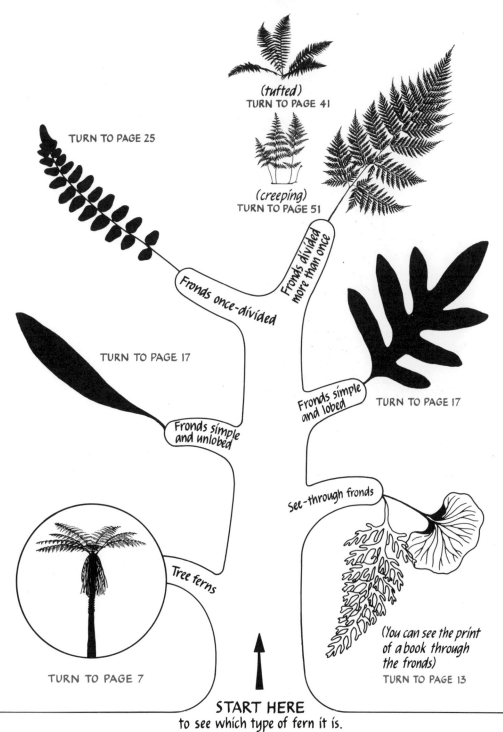

(tufted)
TURN TO PAGE 41

TURN TO PAGE 25

(creeping)
TURN TO PAGE 51

Fronds divided more than once

Fronds once-divided

TURN TO PAGE 17

Fronds simple and lobed

TURN TO PAGE 17

Fronds simple and unlobed

See-through fronds

Tree ferns

(You can see the print of a book through the fronds)
TURN TO PAGE 13

TURN TO PAGE 7

START HERE
to see which type of fern it is.

GENERAL KEY

Mamaku
Black Tree Fern
Cyathea medullaris

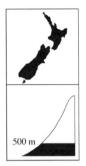

500 m

Size: Trunk up to 20 m tall; *fronds up to 5 m long.*

Features: Tree fern with *flattish oval frond scars* on the trunk. *Frond stalks black and very thick.* Fronds arching. Dead fronds mostly fall but can form an untidy skirt, especially on young plants.

Where: Native to New Zealand and several Pacific Islands. Particularly common in damp forest gullies.

Several Māori uses of this, our largest tree fern, are known. The white pith of the trunk and branches was an important food but is exceedingly slimy unless first steamed in a hāngi. The flavour improves if the pith is then dried.

This same pith has been widely used either raw or cooked as a poultice for sores and wounds, and the reddish gum taken internally for worms and diarrhoea.

In constructing kūmara pits, the fibrous cone of matted aerial roots at the base of the mamaku trunk was split into slabs to form a rat-proof lining.

Cultivation: Easy; fast-growing. Needs watering in dry weather plus shelter from wind and frost. Old fronds left hanging help retain moisture.

LIFE SIZE

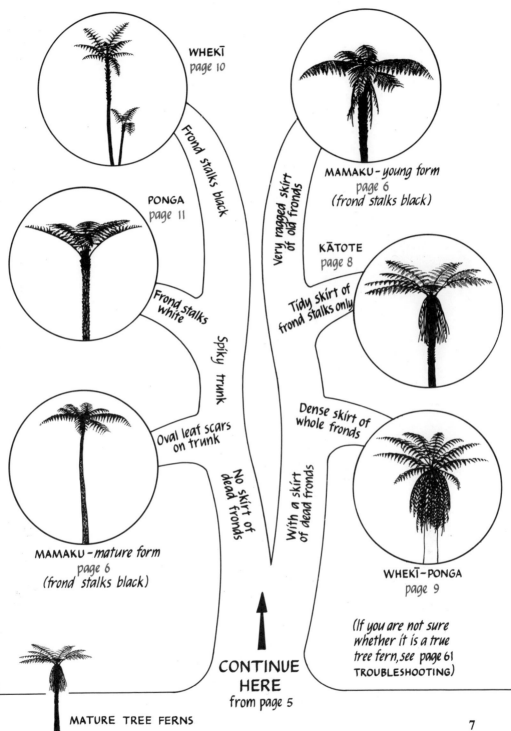

WHEKĪ
page 10

Frond stalks black

MAMAKU – *young form*
page 6
(frond stalks black)

Very ragged skirt
of old fronds

PONGA
page 11

KĀTOTE
page 8

Frond stalks
white

Tidy skirt of
frond stalks only

Spiky trunk

Oval leaf scars
on trunk

Dense skirt of
whole fronds

No skirt of
dead fronds

With a skirt
of dead fronds

MAMAKU – *mature form*
page 6
(frond stalks black)

WHEKĪ – PONGA
page 9

(If you are not sure
whether it is a true
tree fern, see page 61
TROUBLESHOOTING)

**CONTINUE
HERE**
from page 5

MATURE TREE FERNS

7

The skirts of dead fronds will depend also on how sheltered the tree fern is.

Kātote
Soft Tree Fern
Cyathea smithii

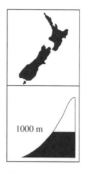

1000 m

Size: Trunk up to 8 m tall; fronds to 2.5 m long.

Features: Tree fern with *very soft, pale horizontal fronds* that leave a distinctive *short skirt of dried stalks* on older trees.

Where: Common in colder and wetter forests, especially at higher altitudes and in the far south. Native only to New Zealand.

South Island Māori ate the cooked heart of kātote. Herries Beattie, writing in 1920, described it as 'a good feed [that] might make good jam – it [has] a sweet taste', but Thomas Brunner, while on his South Island expedition of 1847, called it 'far from palatable, and exceedingly indigestible' (though Brunner was probably describing the raw heart).

Kātote has developed an interesting chemical advantage in the struggle for light and nutrients in the forest: it produces a substance that, while allowing competing seeds to germinate, is sometimes capable of reducing the growth of their roots.

Cultivation: Grows best where moist and cold; needs shelter from wind and frost when young. Otherwise hardy.

LIFE SIZE

Whekī-Ponga
Dicksonia fibrosa

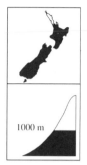

Size: Trunk up to 6 m tall; fronds 1.5–3 m long.

Features: Tree fern with *very thick, soft, fibrous, rusty-brown trunk* and a *heavy skirt* of dead, pale-brown fronds. Many narrow fronds on very short stalks, *harsh* to touch.

Where: In forest and semi-open country. Native only to New Zealand.

The unusually thick trunk is mostly made up of a huge mat of aerial roots. In some areas, these fibrous trunks were split by the Māori to form hard slabs for lining buildings, especially food stores. The fibres, being tough eating for rodents, made the lining effective as a rat-proof barrier.

Whekī-ponga is probably the slowest-growing of New Zealand's tree ferns, there being many specimens that are several hundred years old.

Cultivation: More tolerant of sun and wind than most tree ferns, though it is important to keep the roots protected from drying out. Do not remove dead fronds, as these help protect the fern from wind and sun.

LIFE SIZE

9

Whekī
Rough Tree Fern
Dicksonia squarrosa

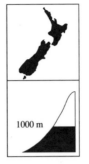

1000 m

Size: Trunk up to 7 m tall; fronds 1.5–3 m long.

Features: Tree fern with slender, often branching,* trunk covered with the *black, peg-like remains of fallen fronds.* Few fronds, scratchy to touch, spreading almost horizontally. Most dead fronds fall, to leave no skirt.

Where: Very common in forest. Native only to New Zealand.

Māori used this fern for forming the walls of their houses, since it lasts well in the ground. For a more decorative effect in guest and meeting houses, the outer surface was hewn clean to show the internal patterning of the trunk. These poles were then used as columns between which to add panels of fern stalks or reeds.

Fences were also made with these trunks to enclose sections of pā. More recently, they have been laid on swampy sections of forest tracks.

Cultivation: Hardy, even sprouting from buried pieces of apparently dead trunk. Tolerates sun and some wind. Roots benefit from mulching.

LIFE SIZE

* The only common tree fern to sometimes have a branching trunk. Also spreads from underground runners, sometimes forming whole colonies.

10

Ponga
Silver Tree Fern
Cyathea dealbata

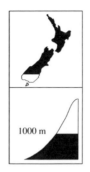

1000 m

Size: Trunk up to 10 m tall; fronds up to 4 m long.

Features: Tree fern with prominent, peg-like frond bases on the trunk. Most distinctive is the *white stalk and underside of mature fronds* – a silvery colouring that appears when the fern is three or four years old.

Where: Common in dry forest and open scrub; rare on the west of the South Island. Native only to New Zealand.

One of New Zealand's national emblems; it appears, for example, on All Black jerseys.

Although the pith was apparently used by Māori as a poultice for skin rashes, more common was the use of the fronds as soft matting on the floors of sitting and sleeping rooms. For this, the fronds were placed silver side down so as to avoid skin irritation from the spores.

Placed silver side up, they provided excellent night-time track-markers, the orientation of the tips indicating direction.

Early European settlers used ponga trunks to make the walls of their huts.

Cultivation: Slow-growing but easy to establish in good, well-drained soil. Needs shelter from wind to look attractive.

LIFE SIZE

11

Raurenga
Kidney Fern
Trichomanes reniforme

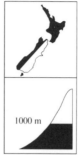

1000 m

Size: Fronds 8–30 cm long.

Features: Creeping ground fern with undivided, *round to kidney-shaped, glossy, translucent*, wavy-edged fronds on long, thin stalks.

Where: Forms mats on forest floor, banks, rocks, or occasionally on tree trunks. Native only to New Zealand.

One of New Zealand's most beautiful ferns, raurenga often appears as a delicate mat of fronds in which little else grows, something it achieves partly through production of a compound that – while allowing competing seeds to germinate – has the power to inhibit the growth of seedling roots.

Another remarkable feature is its tolerance for dry summer conditions, when its fronds curl up tightly to avoid loss of moisture, yet recover fully very soon after rain.

According to Elsdon Best, this was a perfume plant of early Māori.

Cultivation: Very difficult; does not transplant well and is not grown commercially. Suitable only for experts, using a glass case or purpose-built fernery.

LIFE SIZE

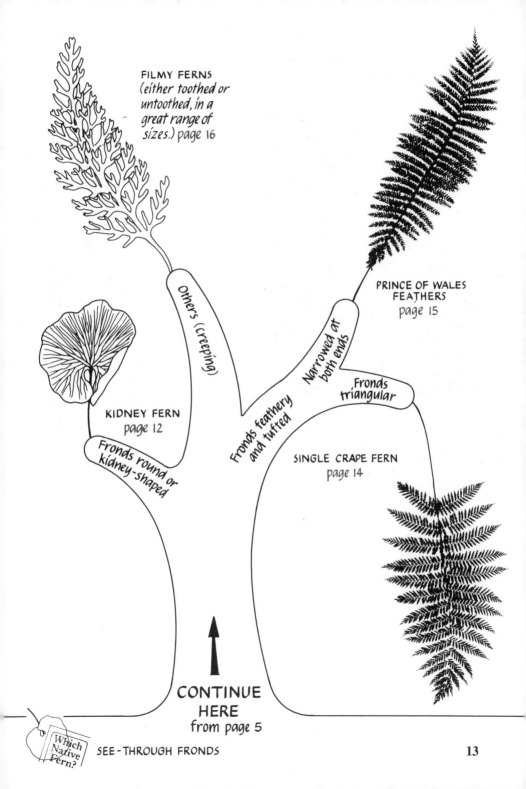

FILMY FERNS
*(either toothed or
untoothed, in a
great range of
sizes.)* page 16

PRINCE OF WALES
FEATHERS
page 15

Others (creeping)

Narrowed at both ends

Fronds triangular

KIDNEY FERN
page 12

Fronds feathery and tufted

Fronds round or kidney-shaped

SINGLE CRAPE FERN
page 14

**CONTINUE
HERE**
from page 5

Which Native Fern?

SEE-THROUGH FRONDS

Heruheru
Single Crape Fern
Leptopteris hymenophylloides

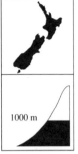

Size: Trunk up to knee-high; fronds 35–150 cm long.

Features: Tufted ground fern, often with a short woody trunk. Fronds very delicate, dark but *translucent* like a filmy fern, *finely divided but flat, and almost triangular*.

Where: Common in damp forest, especially by streams. Native only to New Zealand.

At first glance, this can look like a filmy fern and, like the ferns of that group, most of its fronds are only one cell thick. There are two kinds of crape fern; this, the more common one, is called single crape fern to distinguish it from the more striking and delicate true, or double, crape fern – Prince of Wales feathers. However, its leaflets lie flat in one plane, whereas the leaflets of the double crape lie at right angles to one another, creating a wonderfully ornate feathery plume.

Cultivation: It is difficult to emulate the correct conditions for this fern, which is not available commercially. Best propagated by spores and grown in a glass case or professional fernery with sprinkler system.

LIFE SIZE

14

Heruheru
Prince of Wales Feathers
Leptopteris superba

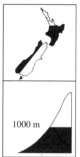

1000 m

Size: Trunk up to waist high; fronds 25–100 cm long.

Features: Tufted ground fern, often with a short woody trunk. Fronds *tapered equally at both ends*, very finely divided. *Fluffy to touch.*

Where: In wet forest, most commonly on the west of the South Island. Native only to New Zealand.

Its remarkably delicate and quite unique feathery appearance has led to this becoming one of New Zealand's favourite cultivated ferns.

Most of the frond is, like the filmy ferns, only one cell thick. But much of its beauty is due to the way in which the finest divisions of the frond overlap each other and stand up at right angles to the frond. Its common names, which include crape fern and double crape fern, are an attempt to describe the textural effect this creates.

Cultivation: Rarely grown commercially and difficult to maintain in good condition. Propagate by spores. Needs rich soil, constant dampness and a cool situation. Slow-growing.

LIFE SIZE

15

Mauku
Filmy Ferns
Hymenophyllum species

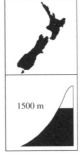

1500 m

Size: Fronds 8 mm–55 cm long, depending on the species.

Features: Mostly creeping, perching ferns with *thin, translucent fronds*.

Where: Common in damp forest or high-rainfall areas, mostly on tree trunks but also sometimes on rocks or on the ground. Most are native only to New Zealand.

New Zealand has almost 30 native filmy ferns. As the name suggests, they have very thin fronds – many only one cell thick. They generally grow in damp bush or in areas of high rainfall, though most are able to cope with long periods of dry weather by curling up tightly. Several have strong chemical defences that are apparently capable of preventing competing plant seeds from germinating or of halting their growth if they do.

Cultivation: None of the species are commercially available. They require constantly humid conditions, a lot of shade and some ventilation. For this, either a glass case or a special fernery with sprinkler system is required.

LIFE SIZE

16

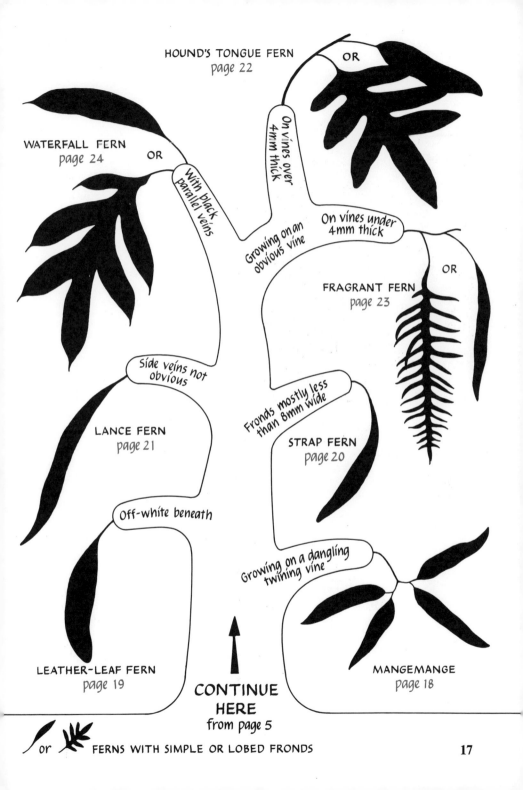

HOUND'S TONGUE FERN
page 22

OR

On vines over 4mm thick

WATERFALL FERN
page 24

OR

With black parallel veins

On vines under 4mm thick

Growing on an obvious vine

FRAGRANT FERN
page 23

OR

Side veins not obvious

LANCE FERN
page 21

Fronds mostly less than 8mm wide

STRAP FERN
page 20

Off-white beneath

Growing on a dangling twining vine

LEATHER-LEAF FERN
page 19

**CONTINUE
HERE**
from page 5

MANGEMANGE
page 18

or FERNS WITH SIMPLE OR LOBED FRONDS

Mangemange
Bushman's Mattress

Lygodium articulatum

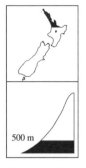

Size: Leaflets 4–10 cm long.

Features: *Loosely climbing* fern with long, wiry, twisting stalks reaching into the tops of trees. Side stalks fork 2–3 times, ending in long, strap-like leaflets. Spore-bearing leaflets look like bunches of small green flowers.

Where: Common in lowland forest. Native only to New Zealand.

The fern's European name comes from the use by Pākehā settlers of the corkscrew-like coils of the climbing stems for stuffing bags to make a simple (but reportedly effective) form of spring mattress. Early Māori used these same stems as rope and for holding down the thatch on their whare and to weave into fish-traps. At the point where the stems bend around obstacles, they become so hard and stiff that they would be hardened in a fire and sharpened for use as fish-hooks.

Technically speaking, the whole 'vine' from the ground up is a frond, so that mangemange can truly claim to have one of the longest leaves in the world.

Cultivation: Difficult; does not transplant easily. A fast grower in warm areas. Needs some shade and a support to climb. Not commercially available.

LIFE SIZE

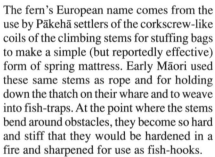

Ngārara Wehi
Leather-Leaf Fern
Pyrrosia eleagnifolia

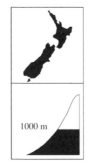

Size: Fronds 3–20 cm long.

Features: Scrambling or climbing fern. Fronds thick and leathery, tongue-like, from almost round to long and strap-like. *Undersides pale and downy. Edges curled under.*

Where: Common on trees and rocks in native forest, exposed coasts and gardens. Native only to New Zealand.

One of the hardiest of ferns, this is as happy growing over a wall or the trunk of an old oak tree in a city garden as in its native forest habitat.

If you have a microscope, it is well worth taking a close look at the dense mat of fine hairs on the undersides of the leaf-like fronds. The individual fawn-coloured hairs form rather pretty star-like shapes, each only 0.5 mm across. These hairs and the unusual fleshiness of the fronds help to protect the fern from loss of water.

Cultivation: Hard to establish but grows well on rocks and walls in dry conditions. If transplanting, take care to keep the growing tip above the soil surface. Not commercially available.

LIFE SIZE

19

Paretao
Strap Fern
Grammitis billardierei

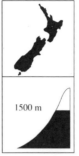

1500 m

Size: Fronds 3–20 cm long.

Features: Tufted perching fern. Fronds *narrow, blunt and strap-like*. Clusters of spore cases on the undersides form a *herringbone pattern*.

Where: Common in forest or scrub on the lower sections of tree trunks, on rocks and occasionally on the ground. Native to New Zealand and Australia.

Known in Australia as finger fern, its botanical name comes from the Greek *gramma* (lines), referring to the arrangement of spore clusters on the fronds, and Jacques Houtou de la Billardière (1766–1834), a French explorer who studied New Zealand plants.

Chemical analysis of the fronds has revealed a small amount of a very powerful insect moulting-hormone compound. This effectively acts as a targeted poison that is believed to have been developed by the plant specifically to protect it against insect damage.

Cultivation: Impossible to cultivate and not worthwhile to attempt transplanting.

LIFE SIZE

Whare-Ngārara
Lance Fern
Anarthropteris lanceolata

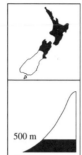

Size: Fronds 7–30 cm long.

Features: Creeps as a mat over tree trunks, forming small *tufts of undivided, thin, fleshy, pointed fronds*. Large brown spore-patches on the undersides of fronds form visible bulges on top.

Where: Common on smooth-barked trees, but also occurs on rocks and banks. Native only to New Zealand.

The European name of this fern refers to the way the fronds are always simple in shape and pointed, like the bladed tip of a lance. Whare-ngārara means 'home of insects'.

Its tender green fronds can form an even carpet over stones, rocks, tree roots and the lower trunks of trees (particularly nīkau), covering quite large areas. In dry weather, fronds hang limply against their support, quite in contrast to the young fronds of fragrant fern. Another feature that distinguishes the two is the lance fern's lack of obvious side veins.

Cultivation: Difficult; not commercially available. Needs a glass case with plenty of humus and damp, shady conditions.

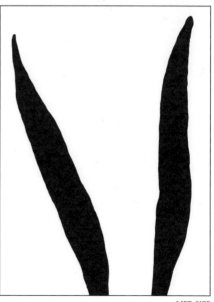

LIFE SIZE

Kōwaowao
Hound's Tongue Fern
Phymatosorus diversifolius

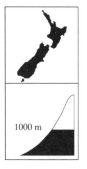

Size: Fronds 8–70 cm long.

Features: Scrambling or climbing fern with a *thick, fleshy, rambling stem*. The long-stalked, *very glossy*, leathery fronds are strap-like when young; later, wide and very deeply lobed.

Where: Very common in forest and scrub on trees, rocks or dry ground. Native to New Zealand and Australia.

The European name is an old one given to several overseas plants with tongue-like leaves. Kōwaowao means to overgrow or choke. This fern is also commonly known as pāraharaha.

According to Elsdon Best, the young fronds were cooked as greens in a hangi and eaten by the Tūhoe people of the Urewera district.

In the same family (Polypodiaceae) is a fern that has been shown to contain a steroidal saponin, osladin, 300 times sweeter than sugar. Another species (the introduced common polypody now growing wild near Christchurch) contains a saponin that is reported to inhibit cancer growth.

Cultivation: Can be grown with shade on well-drained ground or over logs.

Recently renamed *Phymatosorus pustulatus*.

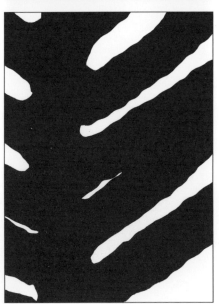

LIFE SIZE

Mokimoki
Fragrant Fern
Phymatosorus scandens

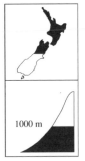

1000 m

Size: Fronds 13–60 cm long.

Features: Scrambling or climbing fern with a *wiry, rambling stem*. The dull, thin fronds are strap-like when young, becoming deeply lobed into up to 20 pairs of leaflets.

Where: Common in forest on trees, rocks or damp ground. Native to New Zealand and Australia.

When fresh, this fern smells of freshly cut grass, but after drying, it emits a strong and lasting sweet marzipan-like fragrance. Mokimoki was used by Māori to scent hair and body oil, make sachets for wearing around the neck or for perfuming a house when guests were expected. The chemistry of its perfume has not so far been investigated.

A useful feature to distinguish the young fronds of fragrant fern from those of lance fern is their dark, net-like veins.

Cultivation: Grows best in shade on damp ground with a tree to climb. Not often available commercially and almost impossible to raise from spore.

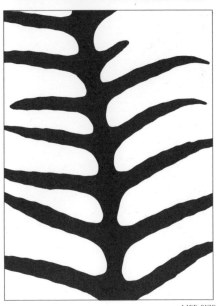

LIFE SIZE

23

Peretao
Waterfall Fern

Blechnum colensoi

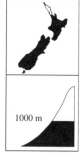

Size: Fronds 16–60 cm long.

Features: Creeping ground fern. Dark, shiny, long-stalked fronds, undivided or divided once into a few leaflets only. Spores on separate shrivelled-looking fronds.

Where: Common *hanging* along *dark, damp forest banks, especially near waterfalls.* Native only to New Zealand.

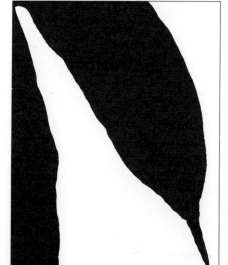

LIFE SIZE

This is a most striking fern, most often noticed clinging to the sides of shaded waterfalls.

Though now known to be native only to New Zealand, peretao is easily confused with similar-looking ferns that grow in the Pacific Islands, the Philippines, Malaysia, India and Australia.

Blechnum species of ferns are unusual in the way they have some fronds that never produce spores and others with shrivelled, thread-like leaflets that specialise is spore production. This feature is a useful clue to their identification.

Cultivation: Best grown in very damp soil in a fairly dark place, with constant dripping water. Can be purchased from some nurseries but hard to maintain.

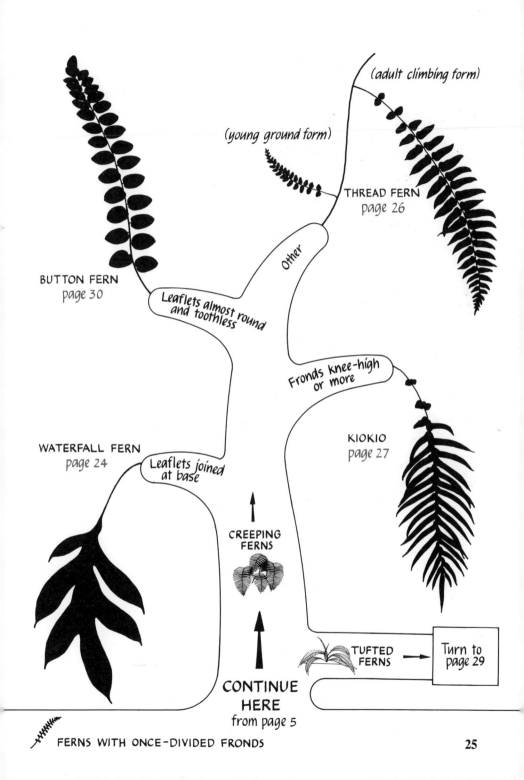

(adult climbing form)

(young ground form)

THREAD FERN
page 26

BUTTON FERN
page 30

Other

Leaflets almost round
and toothless

Fronds knee-high
or more

WATERFALL FERN
page 24

KIOKIO
page 27

Leaflets joined
at base

CREEPING
FERNS

↑

TUFTED
FERNS →

Turn to
page 29

CONTINUE
HERE
from page 5

FERNS WITH ONCE-DIVIDED FRONDS

Pānako
Thread Fern

Blechnum filiforme

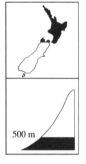

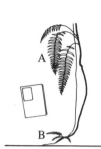

500 m

Size: Creeping fronds 6–30 cm; climbing fronds up to 70 cm.

Features: Creeping and climbing fern. *Ground fronds* (B) *very small with roundish leaflets. Larger, climbing ones* (A) *have very long, pointed leaflets.* Graceful fronds with thread-like leaflets bear the spores.

Where: Common in forest. Native only to New Zealand.

A confusing fern because of its three quite different types of fronds – a feature that makes it unique among New Zealand ferns.

Its common name refers to the attractive wispy thread-like leaflets of the fertile fronds seen growing up on the trunks of trees. These look so different from either the diminutive fronds sprawling over the ground, or the much larger climbing adult ones, that it is hard to believe they belong to the same plant.

The rhizomes of this fern contain ß-sitosterol, the main active ingredient of an American proprietary drug used to lower blood cholesterol levels.

Cultivation: Difficult to propagate and not available commercially. Best in a shady, sheltered spot near a suitable host tree.

LIFE SIZE

(A) Adult, climbing form
(B) Young, ground form

Kiokio
Palm-Leaf Fern
Blechnum species

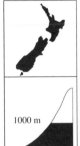

1000 m

Size: Fronds 30–320 cm long.

Features: Large, creeping ground fern. Leaflets strap-like and very finely toothed. Spores on separate, rather shrivelled-looking fronds. New growth *tinged pink or red.*

Where: Very common on road and track cuttings, gullies and cliffs, in scrub and swamps. Native only to New Zealand.

This is one of the plants used by early Māori to wrap their vegetable food to add flavour during hāngi cooking. The fiddleheads themselves can be eaten; they have a mild taste that improves with cooking and flavouring.

Kiokio is cultivated partly for the striking pinkish tinges on the new growth, caused by the presence of flavonoids – the fern's equivalent of sunburn cream.

Cultivation: Though very hardy, prefers damp, shady places. Can easily become a weed. Transplants easily and is best grown on a bank where its long fronds can hang to good effect.

Also well suited for growing in pots and hanging baskets, indoors or out. Available from nurseries.

Blechnum 'kiokio' has, until recently, wrongly been known as *Blechnum capense*. A valid botanical name has yet to be decided.

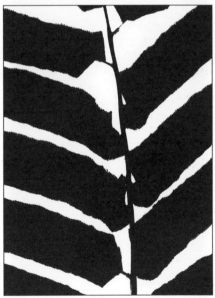

LIFE SIZE

27

Pākau
Gully Fern
Pneumatopteris pennigera

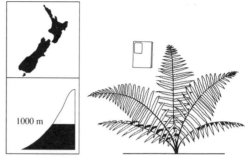

Size: Slender trunk to waist-high; fronds 35–175 cm long.

Features: Tufted ground fern, sometimes forming a short thin trunk. Its brown-stalked, *pale, dark-veined fronds* have 15–30 pairs of long, round-notched leaflets.

Where: Common in damp forest gullies. Native to New Zealand and Australia.

The fronds of this fern were among the flavouring plants used by early Māori to tie around, place under or over, vegetable food in hāngi (earth cooking pits). According to Elsdon Best, Tūhoe Māori of the Urewera district also ate the young fronds. Late last century, in the Whangarei district, the scraped roots were reported as being used effectively as poultices for boils.

Sometimes also known as feather fern or pākauroharoha.

Cultivation: Not particular about soil but needs a damp, sheltered, shaded position protected from frost. Transplants well while still small but not generally available from nurseries.

LIFE SIZE

28

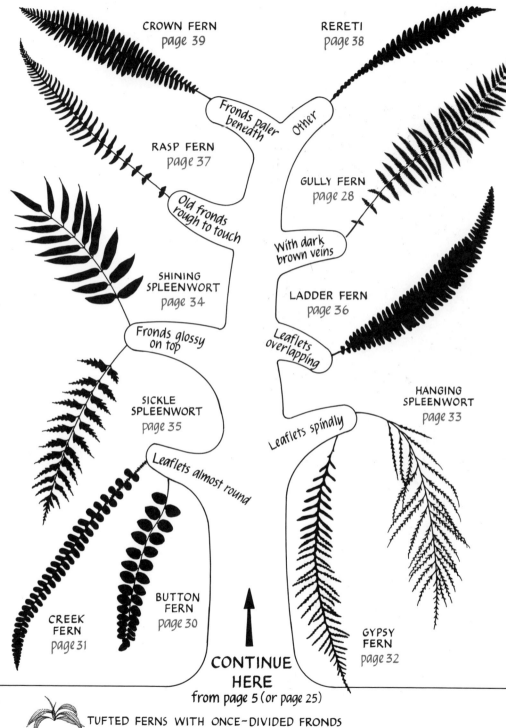

CROWN FERN
page 39

RERETI
page 38

Fronds paler beneath

Other

RASP FERN
page 37

GULLY FERN
page 28

Old fronds rough to touch

With dark brown veins

SHINING SPLEENWORT
page 34

LADDER FERN
page 36

Fronds glossy on top

Leaflets overlapping

SICKLE SPLEENWORT
page 35

HANGING SPLEENWORT
page 33

Leaflets spindly

Leaflets almost round

CREEK FERN
page 31

BUTTON FERN
page 30

GYPSY FERN
page 32

CONTINUE HERE
from page 5 (or page 25)

TUFTED FERNS WITH ONCE-DIVIDED FRONDS

Tarawera Button Fern

Pellaea rotundifolia

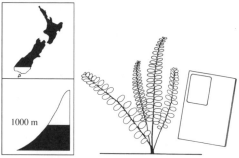

Size: Fronds 20–60 cm long.

Features: Loosely tufted ground fern with very narrow, upright fronds on fine, dark brown stems. *Dark, shiny leaflets on tiny stalks, widely spaced, almost round, sometimes slightly pointed.*

Where: Common in forest in dry rocky places or light scrub. Native only to New Zealand.

The fronds of button fern were among those tested for the remarkable insecticidal compounds (phytoecdysones) that are found in several New Zealand native ferns. Their toxic effect on the larvae of the common house-fly was amongst the highest of those tested – a fact that is expected to have some commercial application.

Cultivation: Prefers a light, rich soil. Requires a certain amount of sunlight (otherwise the leaflets tend to drop off) and is sensitive to over-watering. Popular as a house plant either in a pot or hanging fern basket. Available from nurseries.

LIFE SIZE

Kiwikiwi
Creek Fern
Blechnum fluviatile

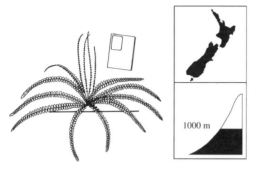

1000 m

Size: Fronds 20–85 cm long.

Features: Tufted ground fern. A dense flattish or drooping rosette of barren fronds with a few upright, spike-like, fertile fronds in the centre. Fronds have 20–60 pairs of *almost round, olive-green*, fairly uniform-sized leaflets.

Where: Native to New Zealand and Australia. Common in damp, shady forest, mostly by streams.

This fern was chewed by Māori to alleviate sore mouths and tongues. More recently, chemical analysis revealed that creek fern contains a small amount of a powerful hormonal insecticide. This substance is thought to protect the fern by mimicking the natural growth hormones that normally trigger developmental changes in insects.

In the late nineteenth century, creek fern found artistic use for what was then known as splash-work – a technique similar to modern-day spray stencilling.

Some compare the look of this fern to a starfish or an octopus.

Cultivation: Easy to grow but needs constant moisture, some shade and rich, well-drained soil. Available from nurseries.

LIFE SIZE

31

Taupeka
Gypsy Fern
Ctenopteris heterophylla

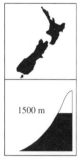

Size: Fronds 5–30 cm long.

Features: Small tufted fern on rocks, trees or banks. Leaflets spindly and leathery, *the longest with deeply jagged edges.*

Where: Common drooping from forest tree trunks, but also (often stunted in size) on wet rocks and banks. Native to New Zealand and Australia.

The botanical name is descriptive: *Ctenopteris* from the Greek *ktenos* (comb), and *pteris* (fern); *heterophylla* from the Greek *heteros* and *phullon* – with differing leaves. The fronds vary a great deal, but all have the appearance of a double-sided comb.

In Australia, this species is known as gypsy fern, most likely from the remarkable range of situations in which it grows: it is found through the entire length of New Zealand from subalpine scrub and Westland rainforest to inhospitable rock crevices on Rangitoto Island.

Cultivation: Difficult; transplanting is not recommended. Not available from nurseries.

LIFE SIZE

Makawe
Hanging Spleenwort
Asplenium flaccidum

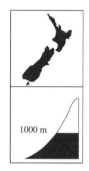

1000 m

Size: Fronds 10–125 cm long.

Features: Tufted perching fern. Fronds very distinctive; leathery, spindly and pale, usually *drooping rather limply.*

Where: Common in forest, even on exposed coasts, mostly perching in trees but also occurs as more erect tufts on the ground or rocks. Native to New Zealand and Australia.

Makawe translates from Māori as 'hair of the head, or ringlets'. 'Hanging' denotes the way this fern usually grows in trees to satisfy its need for light. 'Spleenwort' (an old English name for *Asplenium* ferns generally) refers to a reputation dating back to the first century AD of one species (*A. ceterach*) in healing enlarged spleens, liver and kidney complaints. (The correct pronunciation, incidentally, of 'wort' in such names is *wert*.)

Also commonly known as ngā makawe o Raukatauri.

Cultivation: Available from nurseries and easy to transplant. Does best in very rich soil, with room for the fronds to droop. Suited to growing in hanging baskets and pots. Don't over-water. Beware of slugs, snails and aphids.

LIFE SIZE

33

Huruhuru Whenua
Shining Spleenwort
Asplenium oblongifolium

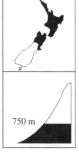

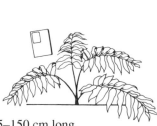

750 m

Size: Fronds 15–150 cm long.

Features: Large tufted fern with very glossy fronds. Leaflets pointed with fine teeth. The brown *herringbone pattern* on the underneath of mature fronds is distinctive.

Where: Common on coastal cliffs, in scrub and forest, usually on ground but also on trees. Native only to New Zealand.

'Altogether glowing' is a translation of the Māori name. The young, curled shoots were eaten by early Māori as greens and were described by one of the early missionaries, William Colenso, as 'very succulent and mucilaginous'. Nowadays the fern is more often eaten by goats and deer.

Appreciated for its fresh appearance in gardens. Indeed, courtesy of a Mr John Edgerley, it reached the Royal Botanic Gardens at Kew in London as early as 1842.

Cultivation: Available from nurseries. Hardy, preferring dappled sunlight. It grows either in deep leaf mould or on old logs. An attractive basket plant, either indoors or out. Beware of slugs and do not over-water.

LIFE SIZE

34

Petako
Sickle Spleenwort
Asplenium polyodon

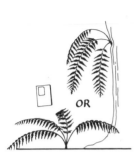

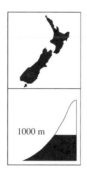

1000 m

Size: Fronds 25–140 cm long.

Features: Large tufted fern, usually hanging from trees. Few graceful, arching fronds, glossy above, with *shaggily and deeply toothed* leaflets.

Where: Commonest on trees or logs in the north; on ground in the south. Native to New Zealand, Madagascar, Asia, the Pacific Islands and Australia.

The original spleenwort that gives this group of ferns its name is described in Dioscorides's *De materia medica* (first century AD) as having the power to cure enlarged spleens, as well as complaints of the liver and kidneys.

'Sickle' refers to the arching shape of the hanging fronds (also of the leaflets). Its unusual grace caught the attention of Victorian plant collectors inspired by the fern craze that swept England in the 1820s and 1830s. Not surprisingly, it has remained a popular fern to cultivate.

Cultivation: Available in nurseries but not easy to establish. Prefers well-drained soil and dappled light. Good as a basket or pot plant.

LIFE SIZE

35

Ladder Fern
Nephrolepis cordifolia

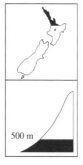

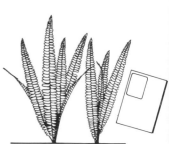

Size: Fronds 45–125 cm long.

Features: Tufted ground fern spreading by runners, with *upright*, brittle, sword-like fronds of *more than 50 pairs* of simple, toothed leaflets.

Where: Commonly grown in northern gardens, but now spreading in the wild. Introduced to New Zealand from the tropics.

There are two kinds of wild ladder fern in New Zealand – one native and found only near hot pools in the thermal regions of the North Island; the other – larger, glossier and widely grown in northern gardens – now spreading (sometimes aggressively) in the wild.

This much more common introduced species bears small potato-like tubers that have been used for food in some countries, including Nepal. Alternative common names for it include fishbone fern, herringbone fern, sword fern and tuber sword fern.

Cultivation: Very easy to grow from runners and tubers in sunny, well-drained spots, but beware of its tendency to spread. Also grown in indoor containers and hanging fern baskets.

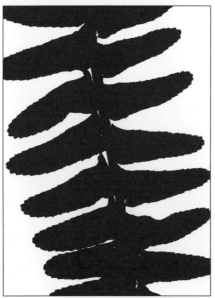

LIFE SIZE

While not native to this country, ladder fern is included in this book because it is so common in the wild that it could easily be thought to be a native fern.

Pukupuku
Rasp Fern
Doodia media

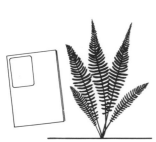

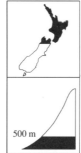

Size: Fronds 15–85 cm long.

Features: Tufted ground fern. Fronds once divided, *rosy-pink when young, rough and raspy when old.*

Where: Commonest in the north, especially in coastal pōhutukawa forest, light scrub, track sides and grassy hillsides – often in full sun. Native to New Zealand and Australia.

Pukupuku translates from Māori as 'gooseflesh', in reference to the surface texture of the fronds. The pink tissue of young fronds contains flavonoids, which protect new growth from ultraviolet damage.

Rasp fern also contains a powerful hormonal insecticide (an ecdysone) that kills the larval stages of insects. While this fact has gone virtually unnoticed here, the commercial applications have attracted keen interest from overseas.

Cultivation: Offered for sale by many nurseries, this fern is easy to transplant and grow. Thrives in partial sun, where its colour shows to best effect. Sensitive to wind. Useful as groundcover.

LIFE SIZE

37

Rereti
Blechnum chambersii

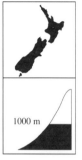

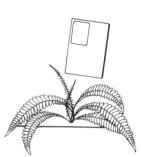

Size: Fronds 15–60 cm long.

Features: Tufted ground fern forming flattish rosettes of fronds, divided into unstalked, finely toothed leaflets. Spores on separate, rather shrivelled-looking fronds.

Where: Common in damp forest, especially along stream banks. Native to New Zealand, Australia, possibly also Fiji, Samoa and Tahiti.

Early Māori collected the young fronds for steaming in hāngi cooking pits as a form of greens.

In Australia, it is appropriately known as lance water fern and is known to have significant insecticidal properties – undoubtedly developed by the fern as part of its defensive mechanism. The hormone involved has the power to upset developmental changes in the growth of insects but is apparently quite harmless to other animals, including humans.

Another common Māori name for this fern is nini.

Cultivation: Hardy. Grows best in the same conditions where it is naturally found: damp with a good amount of shade. Hard to keep looking good.

LIFE SIZE

Piupiu
Crown Fern
Blechnum discolor

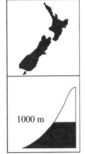

1000 m

Size: Trunk up to waist-high; fronds 25–120 cm long.

Features: Tufted ground fern with an erect crown of fronds, *paler on the undersides*. Separate, rather shrivelled, more erect fronds bear the spores. Also spreads from runners to form colonies.

Where: Common in drier and more open forest. Native only to New Zealand.

This one of the few ferns to survive browsing by possums and deer, a fact thought to be due to the unusually high concentration of astringent-tasting tannins (over 14 per cent by weight) present in the young fronds.

The bent-over fronds have often been used as emergency track-markers – their pale undersides are visible even at night.

In the North Island, crown fern is more common at high altitudes, often forming the main undergrowth in open beech forest and scrub.

Cultivation: Available from nurseries. Small plants transplant well and grow quickly. Hardy, but prefers some shade in rich, damp, well-drained soil. Will grow in a container but does not flourish indoors.

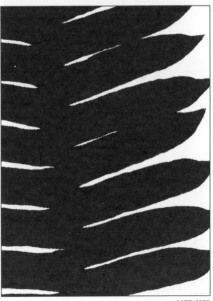

LIFE SIZE

39

Para
King Fern
Marattia salicina

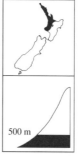

500 m

Size: Fronds up to 4 m long.

Features: Huge, tufted ground fern, with *unusually large, heavy, dark, glossy fronds*, divided into long, strap-like leaflets. Stalks clasping at base, with large, ear-like lobes.

Where: In heavy forest. Once common, but now found only in the odd dark gully. Native to New Zealand and Australia.

Though not common now in the wild, king fern is widely grown in gardens. Its other common names – horseshoe fern and potato fern – refer to the horseshoe-like bracts that were once cut from the underground stems as an important food of early Māori. These were cooked and are said to taste similar to potato. Its rarity, due in part to the appetite of wild pigs, and the fact that one person can eat in one day the growth of five years, nowadays prohibits its culinary use.

Cultivation: Best in rich damp soil with plenty of shade and shelter in areas free of frost. Suited to growing in a tub for either indoor or outdoor use. Hard to grow from spore but available from some nurseries.

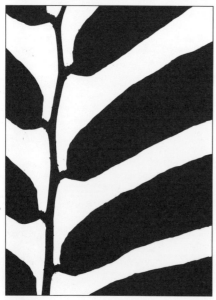

LIFE SIZE

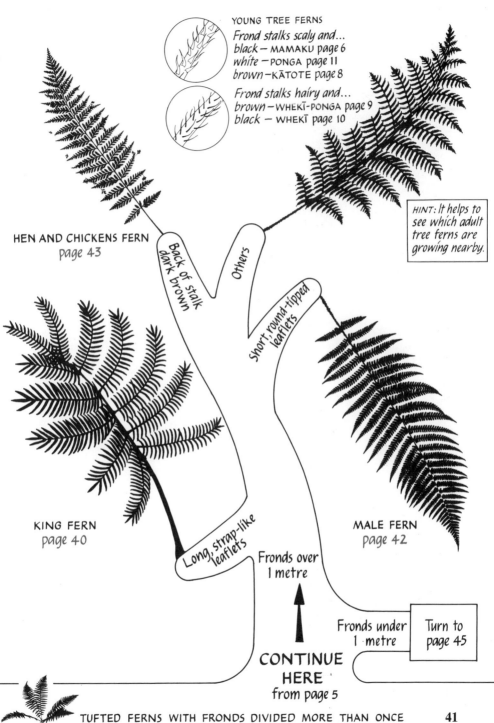

YOUNG TREE FERNS
Frond stalks scaly and...
black — MAMAKU page 6
white — PONGA page 11
brown — KĀTOTE page 8

Frond stalks hairy and...
brown — WHEKĪ-PONGA page 9
black — WHEKĪ page 10

HINT: *It helps to see which adult tree ferns are growing nearby.*

HEN AND CHICKENS FERN
page 43

Back of stalk dark brown

Others

Short round-tipped leaflets

KING FERN
page 40

MALE FERN
page 42

Long, strap-like leaflets

Fronds over 1 metre

Fronds under 1 metre

Turn to page 45

CONTINUE HERE
from page 5

TUFTED FERNS WITH FRONDS DIVIDED MORE THAN ONCE   **41**

Male Fern
Dryopteris filix-mas

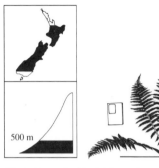

500 m

Size: Fronds 40–165 cm long.

Features: Tufted ground fern. Fronds *paler below*. Stalk covered with wispy scales. Leaflets toothed, rounded at the end.

Where: Common and spreading, particularly in waste ground and forest over much of Canterbury. Introduced to New Zealand from northern temperate countries.

The fern's common name refers to the ancient belief that this was the male counterpart of lady fern (a related fern also spreading in the Christchurch area). For at least 18 centuries the dried underground stems of male fern have been used to rid people of intestinal worms, a property it has because of the presence of oleoresin, which paralyses both the voluntary muscles of the intestine as well as the equivalent contracting tissue of the tapeworm.

In France, the shoots of this fern are boiled as a vegetable.

Cultivation: Favours moist soil under shade in a cool climate. Fronds die off in the winter. Take care not to let this fern spread.

LIFE SIZE

While not native to this country, male fern is included in this book because it is so common in the wild that it could easily be thought to be a native fern.

Mouku
Hen and Chickens Fern
Asplenium bulbiferum

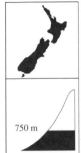

750 m

Size: Fronds 20–155 cm long.

Features: Tufted ground fern. *Stalks and midribs dark brown below, green above.* Fronds feathery, and often recognised by *young plants growing on the upper surface.*

Where: Forest throughout the country. Native to New Zealand and Australia.

The common name of this fern refers to its habit of sprouting young plants from its fronds. These take root once the old frond drops to the ground, but the fern also produces spores in the usual way.

The succulent young unexpanded shoots were cooked and eaten by early Māori and taste rather like asparagus. Tūhoe people also used the fronds for making mat-like bed blankets.

The plant's survival in some areas is threatened by goats and deer.

Cultivation: Commercially available but also easily grown from the young plantlets, so long as at least a part of the old frond is left attached. Prefers damp humus in shade and grows well indoors as a pot plant. The 'hen and chickens fern' grown in gardens is often not the native one but an attractive hybrid.

LIFE SIZE

43

Maukurangi
Miniature Tree Fern
Blechnum fraseri

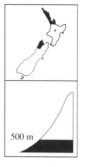

500 m

Size: *Very slender trunk to waist-high*; fronds 25–60 cm long.

Features: Fronds dark, glossy and leathery, with *triangular teeth along the central stalk*. Spores on separate, finer fronds with longer stalks.

Where: A common forest fern in dry forest and scrub. Native to New Zealand, Indonesia and the Philippines.

Although quite unrelated to the true tree ferns, this distinctively primordial-looking plant is often referred to as the miniature tree fern because of the bonsai-like similarity of its shape. It is not surprising, then, to find such a striking and compact fern appearing early last century in the Royal Botanic Gardens at Kew in London. It was one of several to have been sent there in the 1830s or 1840s by the missionary William Colenso, who was a keen naturalist.

Cultivation: Difficult to grow from spore and not easy to establish, but plants are available from some nurseries. Grows quickly in warm weather if given a fair amount of light and well-drained soil. Makes an interesting groundcover.

LIFE SIZE

44

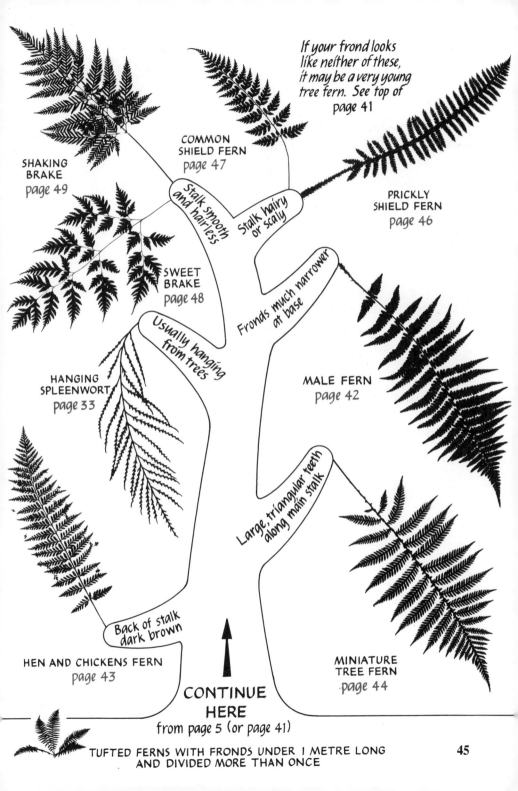

If your frond looks like neither of these, it may be a very young tree fern. See top of page 41

SHAKING BRAKE
page 49

COMMON SHIELD FERN
page 47

PRICKLY SHIELD FERN
page 46

Stalk smooth and hairless

Stalk hairy or scaly

SWEET BRAKE
page 48

Fronds much narrower at base

Usually hanging from trees

HANGING SPLEENWORT
page 33

MALE FERN
page 42

Large, triangular teeth along main stalk

Back of stalk dark brown

HEN AND CHICKENS FERN
page 43

MINIATURE TREE FERN
page 44

CONTINUE HERE
from page 5 (or page 41)

TUFTED FERNS WITH FRONDS UNDER 1 METRE LONG
AND DIVIDED MORE THAN ONCE

Pūniu
Prickly Shield Fern
Polystichum vestitum

Size: Trunk to waist-high; fronds 30–150 cm long.

Features: Tufted ground fern. Its long, narrow, prickly fronds are made up of small leaflets, dark and shiny above, paler below. *Stalks thick and very densely covered in large, dark scales.*

Where: Native only to New Zealand. In forest, scrub and tussock. Very common in the south.

Gwen Skinner recommends the culinary use of shield fern fiddleheads: 'They lend flavour to stews and casseroles and can be put into the pot to boil with meat – particularly beef pot roasts.' However, with so little native forest now left intact, it would be better to limit the fern's use to emergency survival rather than garnishing.

This is one of the many native plants to have suffered badly from browsing deer and goats.

Cultivation: Not particular about shade but likes the cold and does best in deep leaf-mould or peat. Available from nurseries.

LIFE SIZE

46

Pikopiko
Common Shield Fern
Polystichum richardii

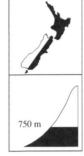

750 m

Size: Fronds 20–85 cm long.

Features: Tufted ground fern. Few fronds, dark, shiny and leathery, on black, wiry stalks with short, hair-like scales. Coastal plants are more fleshy.

Where: Common in coastal areas but also found inland on rocks or ground in scrub and forest. Native only to New Zealand.

The young fiddleheads were, and still are, cooked as a green and eaten by many Māori. There are reports of them being eaten boiled with meat or bacon bones. More recently, they have been recommended cooked as asparagus and served with melted butter on toast or simply as a vegetable. Nowadays, with the survival of our native forest threatened, it would be hard to justify treating them as anything more than an emergency survival food.

Cultivation: Available from nurseries. Hardy. Very easy to grow and useful in gardens. Though not particular about shade or soil, it is likely to need watering in dry weather.

LIFE SIZE

47

Titipo
Sweet Brake
Pteris macilenta

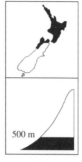

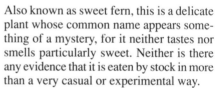

Size: Fronds 35–140 cm long.

Features: Tufted ground fern. Stems yellow-brown. *Fronds delicate and thin*, more open in appearance than shaking brake. *Teeth at tips of lobes.* Veins meet up to form a net-like pattern.

Where: Common in the north in open forest. Native only to New Zealand.

Also known as sweet fern, this is a delicate plant whose common name appears something of a mystery, for it neither tastes nor smells particularly sweet. Neither is there any evidence that it is eaten by stock in more than a very casual or experimental way.

The active principle of a related overseas fern (*Pteris ensiformis*) has proven effective in curing bacillary dysentery in cases where other more conventional treatments failed.

Hold a frond up to the light to see the characteristic net-like pattern of veins.

Cultivation: Available from nurseries. Easy under light shade in damp conditions. Well suited to growing in a container for indoors or out. Prefers a light, friable soil with plenty of leaf-mould.

LIFE SIZE

Turawera
Shaking Brake
Pteris tremula

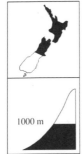

1000 m

Size: Fronds 45–150 cm long.

Features: Tufted ground fern. Stems red-brown. Fronds divided into long *narrow* leaflets, harsher and less open than sweet brake. Veins do *not* form a net-like pattern.

Where: Common in the north in forest, scrub clearings and gardens. Native to New Zealand, Australia and Fiji.

The common name of this fern refers to the way its fronds tend to tremble in a breeze. In summer, says one early writer, 'surveyors cutting lines through the warm sheltered gullies in which it abounds, often find the smell so strong as to be unpleasant, and I have heard it called the "stinking fern" on this account, though many people rather like the scent'. It is fast-growing and unpalatable to stock.

Hold a frond up to the light to see the lack of any net-like pattern of veins.

Cultivation: Available from nurseries and flourishes in most soils. Tolerates direct sunlight, even growing well indoors. Transplants easily but has a short life-span of about three or four years. A common weed.

LIFE SIZE

49

Karuwhai
Climbing Shield Fern
Rumohra adiantiformis

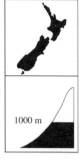

Size: Fronds 20–85 cm long.

Features: Climbing fern. Fronds light with dark veins, leathery, *plastic-like* on very long, grooved stalks. *Round, jet-black spore patches* underneath mature fronds.

Where: Common on forest trees, especially tree ferns. Native to most Southern Hemisphere countries, including New Zealand.

Also occasionally (and appropriately) known as leathery shield fern. Its name refers to the conspicuous round, shield-like spore-case covers on the undersides of fertile fronds.

This is one of several native ferns to contain an ingenious insecticidal compound that mimics developmental hormones in insects. The compound is powerful enough in small quantities to trigger inappropriate changes in the insect's growth, killing any insect unfortunate enough to try to eat it.

Cultivation: Not available commercially. Slow and difficult to grow. Prefers cool, shade and damp. Does best on a tree-fern trunk but also good in a hanging basket.

LIFE SIZE

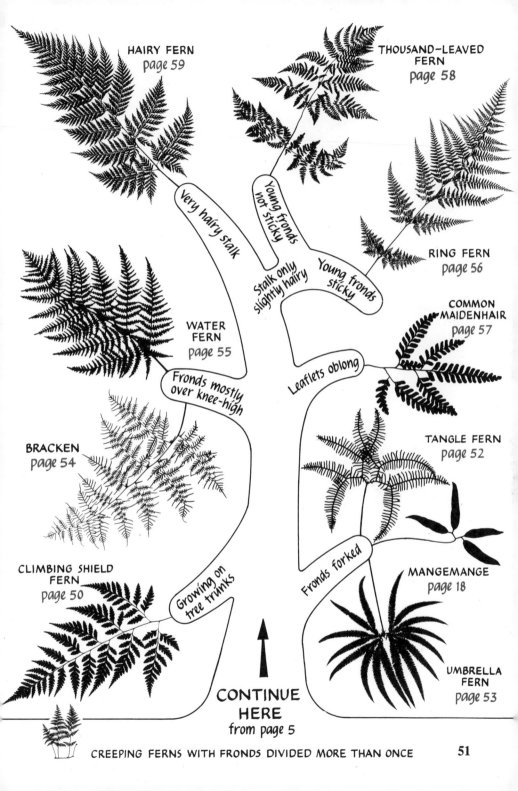

HAIRY FERN
page 59

THOUSAND-LEAVED
FERN
page 58

RING FERN
page 56

Very hairy stalk

Young fronds not sticky

Stalk only slightly hairy

Young fronds sticky

COMMON
MAIDENHAIR
page 57

WATER
FERN
page 55

Leaflets oblong

Fronds mostly over knee-high

TANGLE FERN
page 52

BRACKEN
page 54

CLIMBING SHIELD
FERN
page 50

Growing on tree trunks

Fronds forked

MANGEMANGE
page 18

UMBRELLA
FERN
page 53

CONTINUE
HERE
from page 5

CREEPING FERNS WITH FRONDS DIVIDED MORE THAN ONCE

51

Waewaekākā
Tangle Fern
Gleichenia dicarpa

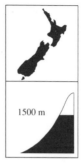

1500 m

Size: Up to about waist-high.

Features: Creeping ground fern with *rough interlacing fronds* on erect red-brown stalks in 1–5 tiers, each tier forked 3–5 times.

Where: Common in swampy areas and poor soil, often in open scrubland. Native to New Zealand, Australia, New Caledonia, New Guinea and the Philippines.

'Footprint of the kākā' in Māori; also known as swamp umbrella fern, though it does grow on dry ground, too. Attractively used in flower arranging.

No Māori uses are known, but a related fern (*Dicranopteris linearis*)* has many applications in Malaysia. Its oldest and strongest stems are sharpened to a resistant point for pens or woven into mats and partition walls in houses, durable fish-traps, stool and chair seats, pouches and long-lasting caps, or twisted together to provide rough ropes.

The name waewaekākā is also used for the very similar-looking *Gleichenia microphylla*.

Cultivation: Difficult to establish and not commercially available. As in nature, tangle fern prefers poor, wet, acid soil, with a fair amount of light.

LIFE SIZE

* This fern is also found in New Zealand but only by hot springs in the North Island.

Waekura Umbrella Fern

Sticherus cunninghamii

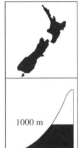

1000 m

Size: To waist-high; 25–60 cm wide.

Features: Creeping ground fern with drooping, umbrella-like fronds, *whitish below*, rising in up to 3 tiers, each forking 3–4 times in *starfish-like patterns*.

Where: Common (except in the far south) in dry, open forest and roadside banks. Native only to New Zealand.

The common name of this fern refers to the flat, spreading shape of the fronds. Several other names are used, a rather beautiful Māori one being tapuwae kōtuku – footprint of the white heron – another reference to the frond's graceful, spreading shape.

　　Tests have revealed small but effective amounts of insecticidal ecdysones, which imitate hormones normally used by insects to signal their growth changes. When eaten by the insect, these compounds set off inappropriate changes that result in its death.

Cultivation: Hard to propagate or transplant and extremely slow-growing. In fact, this is one of the hardest ferns to grow and is not commercially available for this reason.

LIFE SIZE

53

Rārahu
Bracken

Pteridium esculentum

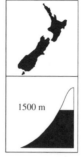

Size: Fronds 20–400 cm long.

Features: Creeping ground fern spreading by underground rhizomes. *Harsh fronds on smooth chestnut-brown stems. Fiddleheads covered in fine, pale-brown hairs.*

Where: Very common everywhere in open places. Native to New Zealand, Australia and many Pacific Islands.

LIFE SIZE

The prepared rhizome, or root-like underground stem (aruhe), of bracken was early Māori's most important wild vegetable food, providing a whitish starch that could be eaten alone, made into cakes, or sweetened with flax nectar or tutu petal juice (minus the highly toxic tutu seeds). Correct preparation of these rhizomes and the furry brown fiddleheads was essential since both are now proven to be cancer-causing when eaten raw.

A light-brown dye can be made from the coiled fiddleheads, using a bichromate of potassium mordant.

Bracken is valuable as the first stage in the birth of native forest.

Also commonly known as rahurahu; the fronds as rauaruhe.

Cultivation: Regarded as a nuisance in gardens because it spreads aggressively by underground rhizomes.

Mātātā
Water Fern
Histiopteris incisa

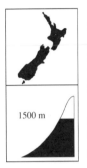

Size: Fronds 40–190 cm long.

Features: Creeping ground fern. Young fronds a distinctive *pea green, and lobed like an oak leaf.*

Where: In moist clearings, edges of forest and along stream banks. Native to New Zealand, and throughout tropical and southern temperate countries.

This fern survives well in the wild since it is one of the few that goats will not eat – the acrid taste of young shoots is enough to show why.

Its common name is appropriate for two reasons: this fern contains a large amount of clear, rather watery sap, and it is often found near water – its fronds often even drooping below the surface of a creek.

Its common Australian name, oak fern, is a reference to the oak-leaf like lobes of the fronds.

The name mātātā is shared by *Paesia scaberula.*

Cultivation: Easy. Tolerates a fair amount of sun, but prefers damp soil. Well suited to growing in a container, especially since it otherwise spreads so easily from its underground stems. Deciduous in the south.

LIFE SIZE

55

Mātātā
Ring Fern
Paesia scaberula

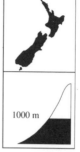

1000 m

Size: Fronds 20–115 cm long.

Features: Creeping ground fern. Its fine, lacy, yellowish-green fronds are often sticky, with *zigzag* chestnut-brown stalks and have a distinctive smell, especially when the sun shines on them.

Where: Common on cleared, sunny, ground. Native only to New Zealand.

Well known to farmers, this fern often grows in colonies in pasture, spreading to form an ever-increasing ring or circle. Equally descriptive is its alternative common name, scented fern, a quality it exhibits when the heat of the sun has been on it a while.

Its essential oil was investigated for perfumery purposes, and shown to contain a sesquiterpene alcohol and the paraffin n-heptacosane. It may one day be grown as a groundcover in wide-spaced stands of pine to provide compounds useful to the perfume industry.

The Māori name mātātā is shared by *Histiopteris incisa*.

Cultivation: Very easy in heavy soil with little shade. Not sensitive to frost. Recommended as a useful groundcover but not often available from nurseries.

LIFE SIZE

56

Puhinui
Common Maidenhair
Adiantum cunninghamii

Size: Fronds 10–35 cm long.

Features: Creeps along the ground. Fronds on long, wiry, shiny, dark-brown stalks. Leaflets *almost oblong, dark green above, blue-green below.*

Where: Common in coastal and lowland forest, on cliffs, banks and among mossy boulders. Native only to New Zealand.

The name 'maidenhair' (given to *Adiantum* ferns generally) dates back at least to the fifteenth century, but it is not known whether it refers to the shimmering grace of the fronds, their fine black hair-like stalks, or to the fern's reputed medicinal properties.

The common European maidenhair is described in the herbal literature of the ancient Greeks and Romans, its many and varied uses including the claim that 'it maketh the hair of the head or beard to grow that is fallen and pulled off'.

Cultivation: Available from nurseries. Easily grown from a clump of underground stem in shaded, moist, lime-rich soil. Not so good indoors because of its creeping habit.

LIFE SIZE

57

Huarau
Thousand-Leaved Fern
Hypolepis millefolium

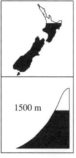

1500 m

Size: Fronds 20–100 cm long.

Features: Creeping ground fern, with open, very finely divided, hairy, wide, diamond-shaped, bright-green fronds.

Where: Large patches common in open or lightly shaded areas. At high altitudes in the north, but down to sea level in the south. Native only to New Zealand.

One of New Zealand's very few deciduous native ferns, its fronds are often regarded as one of our most beautiful. It forms a striking carpet in open beech forest, especially at high altitudes.

Like so many native ferns, it protects itself from insect damage by mimicking a moulting hormone normally found in insects but which, when eaten in quantity, upsets the chemistry of the insects sufficiently to kill them. The poison is ingenious in that it is quite impossible for the insect to adapt a defence.

In the Fiordland winter, when the fronds of this fern have withered away, the starchy rhizomes become an important food of the tākahe.

Cultivation: Prefers damp, light soil and cool conditions. Because it spreads rapidly and soon dies back to look ragged, this fern is not often cultivated.

LIFE SIZE

58

Tuakura
Hairy Fern
Lastreopsis hispida

750 m

Size: Fronds 30–100 cm long.

Features: Creeping ground fern, with harsh, five-angled, finely divided fronds. *Stalks thickly covered in long, black, bristle-like scales.*

Where: Common in forest usually on the ground, though sometimes found on tree trunks. Native to New Zealand and Australia.

Sometimes informally called 'hairy legs', on account of its unusually bristly stem. (Another common and very similar-looking fern – *Lastreopsis glabella* – has smooth stems.)

The fronds of hairy fern contain traces of phytoecdysones – compounds that act as an insecticide protecting the fern from insect damage. The compound ingeniously mimics hormones normally used by the insects to trigger their moulting and metamorphosis, making it quite impossible for the insects to adapt a defence.

Cultivation: Needs shelter and damp with good drainage and dappled sunlight. Available from nurseries and recommended as suitable for growing in a hanging basket.

LIFE SIZE

59

Growing Your Own Ferns

Because ferns have no flowers, their reproductive process was for centuries a complete mystery. Indeed, until their tiny dust-like spores were discovered, it was believed that ferns bore invisible, short-lived flowers only during midsummer's eve, a night credited by the prehistoric Druid religion of northern Europe as a night of mystical powers.

Fortunately for fern growers, this curious mystery has since been solved. For, apart from having no flowers, ferns have neither fruit nor true seeds. And, while all flowering plants are either male or female or both, ferns have no gender at all.

On the underside of most fern fronds you will find a number of dark spots or lines (sori). It is worth looking at these through a magnifying glass; you will see they are made of many small, round bumps (sporangia) that contain the fern's microscopic dust-like spores.

When ripe, thousands of these spores are released and carried by the wind. Some of those that settle in a damp, shady place begin to grow – but not into ferns. Instead, they produce a tiny, heart-shaped plant about 5 mm across (a prothallus). This, too, has no flowers or seeds; instead, it simply has several male and female sex organs (antheridia and archegonia) that each produce lots of sperm cells and one egg.

The male and female organs mature at different times on the same plant, so the wriggling sperms have to swim over the damp surroundings (usually travelling no more than a couple of centimetres) until they find the egg on another sex-organ plant. The sperm fertilises this egg, later to become an adult fern that will replace the dying sex-organ plant. Even the giant mamaku tree fern starts life this way, from a sperm swimming across the forest floor in search of an egg.

Of course, to grow ferns from spores it helps a great deal to know all this. It is important also to know when to collect spores, how to provide the best germinating conditions and how best to sterilise containers and growing medium to keep at bay unwanted algae, fungi and insects. Though guidelines regarding the specific needs of individual ferns are given in the text, for reasons of space it is not possible here to go into more technical advice on the best methods of raising ferns from spores. For this, the best guides are Muriel Fisher's *Gardening with New Zealand Ferns* and Andrew Maloy's *Plants For Free!* (See Selected References.)

It is, in any case, far better for the beginner to purchase young ferns from one of the many nurseries now specialising in native plants. It must be stressed that removing ferns from reserves is neither responsible nor legal; in any case, your chances of success with ferns removed from their forest habitat would be no better than about 20 per cent. It is not hard, then, to see how thoughtless collectors are threatening the survival in the wild of some of our most beautiful ferns.

There are about 50 species of New Zealand ferns that are suited to growing in the garden; most of these are now available from plant nurseries. The key to success with them is always to imitate as far as possible the conditions in which the fern naturally grows. A little familiarity will soon show how specialised most ferns are about the amount of shade and moisture in which they grow best, what kind of ground most suits them and whether they like to grow on, or climb up, the trunks of trees.

Troubleshooting

First, are you sure it is a fern?

When in the bud stage, the fronds of all common New Zealand ferns are tightly coiled like the end of a violin (a 'fiddlehead'). Most either have patches or lines of spore cases on the underside of at least some of the fronds, though some (*Blechnum* species) have instead separate, rather shrivelled looking spore-bearing fronds.

Not a fern, but like a fern

Besides the true ferns are two common groups of what are known as fern allies (distinguished from ferns by their smaller leaves, unbranched veins and by their usually bearing spores on *top* of their leaves).

Fork ferns (*Tmesipteris*) generally hang from the trunks of trees – especially tree ferns – like this:

Club mosses (*Lycopodium*), either hang from trees or scramble loosely over the ground, like this:

Not a tree fern, but like a tree fern

Besides the true tree ferns, six common ferns can produce a small trunk, none of them more than waist-high and none whose trunk cannot usually be grasped in one hand.

Crown Fern (p. 39)   Miniature Tree Fern (p. 44)   Prince of Wales Feathers (p. 15)
Gully Fern (p. 28)   Prickly Shield Fern (p. 46)   Single Crape Fern (p. 14)

If you have trouble matching your frond with the key

1. Are you sure you have chosen a typical *full-grown* frond? Fronds vary a good deal in size, according to where they are growing and how mature they are.
2. Are you sure it is a *wild* fern? Several garden ferns are uncommon in the wild, so are generally not covered in this book.
3. Are you sure the fern is *common*? Less common ferns and those confined to special habitats (e.g., the coast, clefts in rock, bogs, around hot pools) are not included.

If the key is still not working, then take a closer look at the fern:

1. Are you sure whether it is *tufted* (with fronds clustered together in a tight bunch) or *creeping* (with fronds either growing on an obvious vine or scattered along the ground in a line)? Where ferns grow densely enough to form a mat of fronds, it can take careful examination to tell the difference.
2. Are you sure whether the frond is *divided*, or just deeply *lobed*? If the division does not cut all the way to the stalk, then it is described as lobed.
3. Did you remember to start at the *bottom* of the *first* frond key (page 5)?

Selected References

Beever, James. *A Dictionary of Maori Plant Names*. Auckland Botanical Society, 1987.

Best, Elsdon. *Forest Lore of the Maori*. Government Printer, 1942.

Brockie, Robert. *A Living New Zealand Forest*. Bateman, 1992.

Brooker, S. G., R. C. Cambie and R. C. Cooper. *New Zealand Medicinal Plants*. Heinemann, 1987.

Brownsey, Patrick J. and John C. Smith-Dodsworth. *New Zealand Ferns and Allied Plants*. Bateman, 1989.

Burkill, I. H. *A Dictionary of the Economic Products of the Malay Peninsula*. 2 vols. Crown Agents for the Colonies (London), 1935.

Camus, Josephine M. *et al. A World of Ferns*. Natural History Museum Publications (London) 1991.

Chinnock, R. J. and Eric Heath. *Common Ferns & Fern Allies* (Mobil NZ Nature Series). Reed, 1981.

Cooper, R. C. and R. C. Cambie. *New Zealand's Economic Native Plants*. Oxford University Press (Auckland) 1991.

Crowe, Andrew. *Native Edible Plants of New Zealand*. Hodder & Stoughton, 1990.

Dobbie, H. B. *New Zealand Ferns*. Whitcombe & Tombs, 1930 (and other editions).

Field, H. C. *The Ferns of New Zealand*. Willis (Wanganui), 1890.

Fisher, Muriel E. *Gardening with New Zealand Ferns*. Collins, 1984.

Hamlin, Bruce. *Native Ferns* (Nature in New Zealand Series). Reed, 1963.

Heath, Eric and R. J. Chinnock. *Ferns and Fern Allies of New Zealand*. Reed, 1974.

Hutchinson, Amy. *Plant Dyeing*. The Daily Telegraph Co. (Napier), 1941.

Maloy, Andrew. *Plants for Free! – A New Zealand Guide to Plant Propagation*. Shoal Bay Press (Christchurch), 1992.

Martin, R. W. *Ferns For Ferneries*. Betty Simpson (Wanganui), *c*. 1980.

Metcalf, Lawrie. *The Cultivation of New Zealand Plants*. Godwit Press, 1993.

Molloy, Brian. *Ferns in Peel Forest – A Field Guide*. Dept. of Lands & Survey, 1983.

Potts, T. H. *Out in the Open* (includes Classified List of New Zealand Ferns). Lyttelton Times Company, 1882.

Russell, G. B. Insect Moulting Hormone Activity in Some New Zealand Ferns. *NZ Journal of Science* 14: 31–35, March 1971.

Skinner, Gwen. *Simply Living*. Reed, 1981.

Stevenson, Greta. *A Book of Ferns*. John McIndoe, 1954.

Thomson, G. M. *The Ferns and Fern Allies of New Zealand*. Henry Wise (Dunedin) 1882.

Index

Adiantum cunninghamii, 57
Anarthropteris lanceolata, 21
Aruhe, 54
Asplenium bulbiferum, 43
Asplenium flaccidum, 33
Asplenium oblongifolium, 34
Asplenium polyodon, 35

Black Tree Fern, 6
Blechnum capense, 27
Blechnum chambersii, 38
Blechnum colensoi, 24
Blechnum discolor, 39
Blechnum filiforme, 26
Blechnum fluviatile, 31
Blechnum fraseri, 44
Blechnum 'kiokio', 27
Bracken, 54
Bushman's Mattress, 18
Button Fern, 30

Climbing Shield Fern, 50
Common Maidenhair, 57
Common Shield Fern, 47
Creek Fern, 31
Crape Fern, 15
Crown Fern, 39
Ctenopteris heterophylla, 32
Cyathea dealbata, 11
Cyathea medullaris, 6
Cyathea smithii, 8

Dicksonia fibrosa, 9
Dicksonia squarrosa, 10
Dicranopteris linearis, 52
Doodia media, 37
Double Crape Fern, 15
Dryopteris filix-mas, 42

Feather Fern, 28
Filmy Ferns, 16
Fragrant Fern, 23

Gleichenia dicarpa, 52
Grammitis billardierei, 20
Gully Fern, 28
Gypsy Fern, 32

Hairy Fern, 59
Hanging Spleenwort, 33
Hen and Chickens Fern, 43
Heruheru, 14, 15
Histiopteris incisa, 55
Horseshoe Fern, 40
Hound's Tongue Fern, 22
Huarau, 58
Huruhuru Whenua, 34
Hymenophyllum species, 16
Hypolepis millefolium, 58

Karuwhai, 50
Kātòte, 8
Kidney Fern, 12
King Fern, 40
Kiokio, 27
Kiwikiwi, 31
Kōwaowao, 22

Ladder Fern, 36
Lady Fern, 42
Lance Fern, 21
Lastreopsis glabella, 59
Lastreopsis hispida, 59
Leather-Leaf Fern, 19
Leathery Shield Fern, 50
Leptopteris hymenophylloides, 14
Leptopteris superba, 15
Lygodium articulatum, 18

Maidenhair, 57
Makawe, 33
Makawe o Raukatauri, 33
Male Fern, 42
Mamaku, 6
Mangemange, 18

Marattia salicina, 40
Mātātā, 55, 56
Mauku, 16
Maukurangi, 44
Miniature Tree Fern, 44
Mokimoki, 23
Mouku, 43

Nephrolepis cordifolia, 36
Ngārara Wehi, 19
Nini, 38

Paesia scaberula, 56
Pākau, 28
Pākauroharoha, 28
Palm-Leaf Fern, 27
Pānako, 26
Para, 40
Pāraharaha, 22
Paretao, 20
Pellaea rotundifolia, 30
Peretao, 24
Petako, 35
Phymatosorus diversifolius, 22
Phymatosorus pustulatus, 22
Phymatosorus scandens, 23
Pikopiko, 47
Piupiu, 39
Pneumatopteris pennigera, 28
Polystichum richardii, 47
Polystichum vestitum, 46
Ponga, 11
Potato Fern, 40
Prickly Shield Fern, 46
Prince of Wales Feathers, 15
Pteridium esculentum, 54
Pteris macilenta, 48
Pteris tremula, 49
Puhinui, 57
Pukupuku, 37
Pūniu, 46
Pyrrosia eleagnifolia, 19

Rahurahu, 54
Rarahu, 54
Rasp Fern, 37
Rauaruhe, 54
Raurenga, 12
Rereti, 38
Ring Fern, 56
Rough Tree Fern, 10
Rumohra adiantiformis, 50

Scented Fern, 56
Shaking Brake, 49
Shining Spleenwort, 34
Sickle Spleenwort, 35
Silver Tree Fern, 11
Single Crape Fern, 14
Soft Tree Fern, 8
Sticherus cunninghamii, 53
Strap Fern, 20
Swamp Umbrella Fern, 52
Sweet Brake, 48
Sweet Fern, 48

Tangle Fern, 52
Tapuwae Kōtuku, 53
Tarawera, 30
Taupeka, 32
Thousand-Leaved Fern, 58
Thread Fern, 26
Titipo, 48
Trichomanes reniforme, 12
Tuakura, 59
Tuber Sword Fern, 36
Turawera, 49

Umbrella Fern, 53

Waekura, 53
Waewaekākā, 52
Water Fern, 55
Waterfall Fern, 24
Whare-Ngārara, 21
Whekī, 10
Whekī-Ponga, 9